PEBBLES AT THE BEACH
A POETRY COLLECTION

Steven Thomas Dykes

Author's Tranquility Press
Marietta, Georgia

Copyright © 2022 by Steven Thomas Dykes.

All rights reserved. No part of this publication may be reproduced, distributed or transmitted in any form or by any means, including photocopying, recording, or other electronic or mechanical methods, without the prior written permission of the publisher, except in the case of brief quotations embodied in critical reviews and certain other noncommercial uses permitted by copyright law. For permission requests, write to the publisher, addressed "Attention: Permissions Coordinator," at the address below.

Steven Thomas Dykes/Author's Tranquility Press
2706 Station Club Drive SW
Marietta, GA 30060
www.authorstranquilitypress.com

Ordering Information:
Quantity sales. Special discounts are available on quantity purchases by corporations, associations, and others. For details, contact the "Special Sales Department" at the address above.

Pebbles at the Beach /Steven Thomas Dykes
Paperback: ISBN 978-1-957208-75-6
eBook: ISBN 978-1-957208-76-3

Table of Contents

Dedication 7
Acknowledgements 8
Prelude: 9
1. The Birth of Fire 11
2. An Island of Luminous Bliss 12
3. Winds of Destiny 15
4. Heroes 16
5. Blind Man Davis 18
6. Champaign in the Morning 19
7. The Tree 20
8. Seed of Mother Nature 21
9. Falling on Deaf Ears 22
10. Temptress Dressed as an Angel 23
11. Addicted/Momma Help 24
12. to My Best Friend 25
13. Empty House 26
14. Last Sunrise 27
15. The Soul of Capitalism 28
16. The Truth of Mankind 29
17. The Sunday of April 30
18. The Heart of Evil Men 31
19. Cherish Natural Age 32
20. Money/The Tale of Faust 33
21. Run Away Little Boy 34
22. A Flower at Sea 35
23. Rocking Chair/Time 36
24. We'll meet Again 37

25. In the End 38
26. Tequila God 39
27. Love of my Life 40
28. Color of Sadness 41
29. Theater near You 42
30. The Sorrow of June 43
31. The Death of a Wiseman 46
32. Burning the Past 47
33. My Angel of Love 48
34. From Kansas 49
35. Quandary of Love 50
36. The Wind 51
37. Duality 52
38. Whispers of the Sea 53
39. Tired of the Streetlight 54
40. The Great American Love Song 55
41. The Manifestation of Time and Love 56
42. Direction is born 57
43. The Storyteller 58
44. Pick up the Phone 59
45. Flight around the Sun 60
46. A Vacation of Wine 61
47. Winter Song 62
48. Treasure Chest 63
49. Survive 64
50. Memory of her Scent 65
51. The First Snow 67
52. On the Farm 68
53. Café' Stevens 69

54. Gray Sky Turned Blue 70
55. City of Red 71
56. My November Rain... 72
57. 29 Years, 29 Ways 73
58. Real or Fake 74
59. No Country 75
60. Penny in the Well 76
61. The Frost 77
62. And Tonight's Special is... 78
63. She Loves Me 79
64. Onto a New 80
65. Waiting for the Tide 81
66. The Immigrant.. 82
67. Only the Thief 83
68. To Hear Her Footsteps... 84
69. Find Comfort 85
70. Mysterious Nights 86
71. Shooting Star... 87
72. Winter Wind 88
73. Create the Day 89
74. Boy from Kansas 90
75. You 91
76. Chasing a Shadow 92
77. Dawn.. 93
78. The Scent that Lingers 94
79. Recipe for Love 95
80. Knowing Where to End 96
81. Everything... 97
82. I Live in Casablanca 98

83. If I could Have you 99
84. My First Line to You 100
85. The Morning Fire 101
86. Will and Self..102
87. Dressed in Mud...103
88. A Red Heaven 105
89. Sea of Blue 106
90. At Night 107
91. November Rain...108
92. Vernal Equinox 109
93. The End is Close 110
94. Consideration 111
95. The Four Women...112
96. Season of fall 114
97. The Circle of Life 115
98. Temptation...116
99. Feathers 117
100. Blue Eyes 118
101. Beyond Time..119
102. Timeless Age 120
103. Often a Dream 122
104. Conclusion 123
Epilogue..124

Dedication

I wish to dedicate this novel to the sweetest flowers of my life: Betty Jean and Dinah Ann.

"There's no way I can pay you back, but my plan is to understand......you are appreciated",

Tupac Shakur

Acknowledgements

Editor: Dinah Dykes

Cover art: Steven Dykes

Prelude:

"O rose, thou art sick!
The invisible worm
That flies in the night,
In the howling storm;

Has found out thy bed
Of Crimson Joy:
And his dark secret love
Does thy life destroy."

        -William Blake
        "The Sick Rose"

"For here I am in summer, without even knowing spring"

- Verna Zumbrum

1. The Birth of Fire

Standing outside a campfire, the heat causing perspiration
The rubbing of the sticks to spark, was the first human creation
In the first necessity, for God granted us light
He brought down the warmth, in the midst of a summer night

With the month of July, early it begins with celebrating
Without a way to dry the sweat dripping from off my brow
To wipe away, wiping with a dirty towel

Holding onto the past dirt, to create new soil
We dig to discover the life we now foil
In preservation of self, and our conceited ways
For what we know, we simply delay

Rubbing sticks below hay, started the new age
But how can we not preserve the histories stage
That evolved into the era of technology
That spawned fire into electricity.

2. An Island of Luminous Bliss

Are you ready for the moksha-medicine…?

Spaces of living light that pulsed
Close your eyes
To the luminous bliss

That light grew brighter
And understanding deepened,
Dear God,
    Oh,
        Dear God,

Limitless and undifferentiated awareness
Crystalline transparency
God glows and he flames
From an ocean poured of absolute transcendence of the self
    Upon this island,

Pure spirit that was 100 proof
A drink that only the warm indulged
Pure contemplation beyond contingency
Without the context of moral judgment!
OPEN YOUR EYES!
To inner illumination
Like a blind man newly healed!
Confronted with the astonishment of color and light

*The walls of paradise
At the heart of a tropical landscape
The open sea
Enormous horizon
Towered clouds into a pale sky
The still sad music called humanity…*

*Those compositions brought to us by the mystical abyss but still,
There are horrors of pain and vulgarity*
      Cruelty
            Tastelessness
                  Deliberate malice…

*Nordic angels with the faces of baroque saints ignored
Yet,*

*There were faces of lovers reaching their climax
That created one realm
Along with the awareness that we exist alone
For,*
    Nothing is forever!
There is no such thing as infinity!

*Only the mystery of touch
Communicating through skin,
Half in mysterious darkness*

Half glowing with a golden light
That leaves your heart content,
    To be…

Thankful for being alive
Thankful for understanding this knowledge
And,
    Thankful…
        For this island,
            Of luminous bliss.

3. Winds of Destiny

The winds of destiny prevail
From the seven seas
To the mountains of the world
Blowing through your hair with certainty
Without control…

You feel the angels before us
Whispering wisdom
Devouring consciousness
Leading you to the path of righteousness
You walk with hesitation
Following the yellow brick road
Not in Kansas anymore,

You've fallen for the Gods
Six feet deep…

Now,
As death arrives,
You become…
    The winds of destiny.

4. Heroes

Where have all the heroes gone?
The revolutionists, crying for change
With desperation for tomorrow
Where…
    Oh, where…

Why have all the ancient Gods disappeared?
The saviors preaching peace
As the tides roll in,
    Further and further,
Time,
    Passes vastly…
Up in the clouds

I can't come down
Why,
    Oh, why?
With the past playing on an 8mm camera
Black and white,
    Of the dreamer…

And his dream was spoken with crystalline words
A circumference running round and around,
Where have all the heroes gone,
With their dreams still spinning in the air…

You must,
Open your eyes
To see the truth,
  You must,
Open your ears
To hear the sound…

That is where all the heroes pray,
From out of the blindness
Up in the clouds
Removing all prejudices and judgment
That is,
  Where the heroes,
    Are found.

5. Blind Man Davis

Let me tell you a story
      Of Blind Man Davis,
He was born without sight
But he wouldn't trade
      Anything to see
For,
He would rather be blind, homeless and alone…

Still,
      He smiles…

I say, "What's up Blind Man Davis,"
He tells me, "Well, I hear the sky?"
As I walk by
I laugh at his joke
But still,
      I don't understand
           This man…

"Blind Man Davis,"
I asked him, "Why don't you want to see?"
He told me, "Why do you, when you are blind already?"

I smiled, walking by
      Only to turn around to see
           Blind Man Davis,
Winking his eye.

6. Champaign in the Morning

I toast champaign in the morning
To help ease my mind
Living for another day
Inside the shell of society
With the light of the divine

But this toast is, a toast to all
With that dream of heaven at night
Waiting for the sun to rise
So I could see the color of Champaign
That comes with each new day
God's creation, the sunlight.

7. The Tree

The trade wind blows, alas, the tree is bare
Last leaf falling delicately, floating in the air
Without gravity, nature bestows a season's twine
Enjoying the taste of her sweet and red wine

Empty inside, I see the tree a pair
Floating without wings, silent to the air
He is naked and collard, by its texture
The waking sadness, of its completers

The trade wind sings, alas, a song of despair
Left the sight, without a moments contraire
To what we see, and what we hear,
My tree, my tree,
    Alone, my dear.

8. Seed of Mother Nature

The deep seed you plant knowing patience is crucial
Weak upon your knees, touching the soul, burying the unusual
This seed represents my soul, my hierarchy
Awaiting its bloom, yearning for destiny

Two months later, the seed begins to sprout
Beautiful and frail, the green leafs of doubt
It has been born, the path belongs to bloom
So small and sensitive, the path is akin to doom

Waiting with anticipation, for another month
Thirty days I count,
Today is the day I become a man!
I shout,

Running through a sea of golden wheat fields,
to the place of conception, granting its chance for a free meal
With a bucket in hand, I find my sprout
The closer I look, the more I doubt

"This isn't my seed," I shout
"It couldn't be," beyond the doubt
I pondered and walked, a few miles by
Searching and fighting, I learn that the seed was never mine

9. *Falling on Deaf Ears*

I sang, and nobody listened
I painted, but nobody looked
Telling tales of unprediction
To blame, the envious book

Telling tales of intervention and resurrection
In a file trashed with reprehension
The calm of the storm approaches
And my mind and soul feels hopeless

The seed that never grew, the plant I never was
This deed, forever new, my banishment becomes
Fallen into the spirit of the Gods,
Calling the beginning to fear due to cause,

Thy hast, all that hitherto possesses, for its more to define
Why hast, our hitherto, are blessed, in case of your mind
Scripted in a song, dance, and art falling on deaf ears
My clue will belong, chance, and start belonging time past due.

10. Temptress Dressed as an Angel

Eyes green with greed and sinister acts
Her clean lies fool the honorable tracks
Tracing the footsteps of a seductive temptress
Erasing them as her spirit forgives this,

Nature of breaking hearts, and crushing should
Weightless to her torment that's unconcealed
No God to fear, no inferno to dread
The answer is clear, only seconds lead to death

She stole my ghost, then hypnotized my mind
Emptied my pockets, all of my life she could find
Lifeless and alone, I bask in her kiss
Blacker than night, collectively reminiscing

The smile of her beauty, vanishing her soul
Eyes of pure bliss, somehow, turned cold
Remembering her voice, her laugh, and her tears
Wiping them away, stolen, was my innocence of years.

11. Addicted/Momma Help

Momma, momma, please don't take my gun
I won't shoot up, needless I shun
No more pushing, and no more cries
Can't help the lies in my eyes

The dragon I chase only sees red
Is it the blood, or am I already dead
The plunger pushed in with a sigh
A needle I no longer feel or deny

Momma, momma, please don't take away
The heaven on earth, I feel today
Drunken to the point of no return
I can see my destiny, and it's burnt

Momma, momma, I'm begging you, let go of your little boy
I can't stop this chase, playing with this toy
Tag, I am it, but no fast enough to catch anymore
All I can do is forget the past, that's killing your little boy

Momma...
    Momma...

12. to My Best Friend

He travels northward, where the snow amass away
Deep within the path, no chance he was led astray
Wandering through the cold, where the water turns to ice
A lake of strength, he stands alone without fright

Freedom, bliss, he cries to the ancient Gods
Yearning to kiss, his destiny and beyond
Not stopping or even a pause of doubt in his step
His footprints, walking down the path he dreamt

To see beyond his birth, he smiles at the heavens above
I will miss him, and know his plight is forever beloved
From the shadows he once made,
Of my best friend,
No longer afraid,
To search for an end.

13. Empty House

You will never know,
 The daggering pain,
  Of a man lost…

That comes home alone.

14. Last Sunrise

Sing a song,
For,
    Today, I move on...

Putting all my possessions in boxes
It has been three years since I moved back to the home of my birth
Over two decades with the warmth of a blanket called adolescence
I spent it well, and will cherish it all from the language of love
Even when the principles came, and I despised my plight
For I was a bird, afraid to give flight;

But today is the day
That I move from my nest
To build my own home
For my children to rest;

Singing, the morning song,
Of the last sunrise at home
Before my soul becomes one
It is time to live in the now
Far away,
    From the house of the rising sun.

15. The Soul of Capitalism

The simplicity of mind over matter,
*   The task so basic,*
Yet not many can attain complete mind over matter
Or even know that existence holds liberty of the individual

For free-will is the fright, and the exuberance, of all mankind
Being alone, secluded, but only what you cannot afford
Life, and it being, a material possession,
The saddest days of how I grow…

Humans are no longer measured by character, but equity
So selfish, people want to have the best dressed date at the prom
No longer is beauty of the soul measured, t'were I sit collecting dust
A pretty face, I hide, and I run,
For I do not want to become a doll
Made from a factory of shallow enterprise
By the character that lives inside a capitalist society.

16. The Truth of Mankind

The essence of all that surrounds me
Is a force of gravity unto its own creation beyond the contingency
of a holy realm?
Lessons too tall,
Walls of a forest that traps the sun,
Looking up to find my direction
Lost in the enchantment of dissolution
With the lack of water leaving me without a tear to shed
Wanting to cry with these eyes of sand
I become numb as darkness falls, I land…

My mind searches for a high,
Turning on a flashlight,
    Pointing it to my carpet,
        On my hands and knees
            Searching for a speckle of coke,
Please God,
    Oh please…

17. The Sunday of April

It is Sunday, a Sunday in April
The leaves blossom, t'were growth remedies
Behind the trees, of a grander place in time
I hold her hand, and once again, I learn how to fly

A poet's loss of hope, standing still with the wind
Memories dazed or misconstrued we lost substance
I was an officer in the army of enchantment, enticed with misery
My expression was one of darkness, and my truth doesn't hurt

I lost my contention,
    Have I lost my soul?

It is Sunday…
    Sunday in April,
24 years ago today, I was born,

But the day Learned true destiny,
Was the moment of my conception?

18. The Heart of Evil Men

Black as night,
Cold as ice,
A man without a sense of morality
Anything to advance his own plight
The heart of an evil man
Fears no god.

19. Cherish Natural Age

What is withdrawn from the fountain of youth?
Replenished by the evolution of science
You can surgically repair all that you see in the mirror
    But,
        The truth.

20. Money/The Tale of Faust

Those evil deeds we climb,
    I find,
The fact of the matter is
    We live
In a society indulged
    We sold,
    Our soul…

To the price of class,
We must pass,
On the extent,
To cement,
With our morality,
So callously,
Falling in love,
    With the color of green,
        Those evil deeds…

We climb…

But what do we truly find?

21. Run Away Little Boy

Run away, little boy
Hide from your dreams
Dismiss a prophecy
Destined to believe
   The leaves of November,
Runaway, child,
   Free to your conscious,
Run away, little boy
And,
   A man you will find.

22. A Flower at Sea

I am but floating upon the earth
Searching for land,
I am lost amongst this enormous sea
Gone to glory,
a place that I could grow
Into an island of dreams
I yearn to conclude,
Finding soil to become planted,
Growing from the flower I once was,
Into the tree that found land.

23. Rocking Chair/Time

An old man, sitting in his rocking chair
Watching the rain fall, the puddle once glared
From the light, Sun falling after the storm
Rocking back and forth, there once before

The endless days adrift, splashing in the steps
He remembers the days of youth, and never regrets
When he fell in love, when he held his boy from past memories
fell, even with a toy

He played with as a child, reminiscing of his chair
Rocking back and forth, above the clouds, he stares
Awaiting the Sun to fight through the sky
Feeling the eternity of his endless crying eye

An old man,
Rocking back and forth,
Cold and alone, he closes his eyes
Awakening to his destined demise.

24. We'll meet Again

Acknowledgement of fate and sacrifice
Living in an empty house
Not dead, but not alive

A man of wicked consumption
Delusions of day and night, hiding from fate
I only find morality and joy in knowing
This doctrine
This simple nondescript folly
Of the artist and poet named Thomas,
The love and my friend
      That you will soon,
           Meet again.

25. In the End

The all-American prodigy
Born from sweat and blood
He was conceived from a forest of red
Autumn time fell like leaves of change
Remembrance bestowed in pretenses arranged

Sparking a fire that spread to the hearts of humanity
The crossroads he walked granted each step closer to insanity
Not faulting vanity, pride or greed, feet avoiding temptation
To pronounce man's morality in his manifestations

Age brings about closure, and scars let us know we were once alive
Cutting down the branches and vines of bondage to testify
Before God, before all, he vows an oath of cleanliness in life
Of the soul, brought about this decision scorn by a knife

Left to fend off the predators that smell blood
To continue his dance through the deepest of mud
Knowing that it is not where you have been,
It is where you are going,
    In the end.

26. Tequila God

Waking up to a tequila hangover, eating the worm
Falling down the stairs to sleep, dream, and yearn
I find pleasure in the yawning of a new dawn
Onto the next night and beyond

I slap on some soap, while scrubbing my teeth
All I can think, what's left to drink
Noon the clock read, a time awaiting a sip
Showering with a bottle of bourbon, how slowly I forget

In the sand of a drunken lifestyle
I dress myself in clothes expressing tattered smiles
The days of a circular pit, digging with nails
Your fingers bleed, gripping like a snail

For a tequila moon and the howling that comes
What is more in life than the drunken sun?
Shinning the light of inhabitations with diminished health
All for the words granted from the Lord himself.

27. Love of my Life

The day I lost my breath, and fell in love
I recall with photographic clarity and emotional disparity
She walked into my life, and things would never be the same
Her hair golden brown, glowing green eyes that sung the refrain

I took a drink, to build up courage
In the lounge, I came, asking could flourish
This dance we share, replays in my mind
Through generations of time

Loneliness breeds a temptress that leaves a winter breeze
But when I think about holding her, the winds loudly sing
An ocean of solitude, I must endure

Through the past and giving a heart beat
She put her head on my shoulder, she never let go
We kept dancing, until God only knows.

28. Color of Sadness

I turned a turquoise color of sadness
forming a rock of salvation to those you love
You look around at those that dislike their own presence
Most men wish to hold rocks stability,
    The description you sit, starring across the sea,
    I can only wonder, whispers of what's to be,
Night after night,
The color of sadness lives inside of me.

29. Theater Near You

Thinking about you has changed the way I howl at the moon
Drinking to the sunrise, I can't believe I could feel so blue
Yet left brand new, to see beauty in a way never sought
Finally the day had crept up, and left me caught

In a net, like a fish, who is taking his last breath?
Every time I think about your smile, I don't believe
That I have fallen in love, I swore, never, not me
And there is a heaven above, now sure to destiny

Never again, I beg and plead
Not to bend, never lend, my heart to bleed
With a needle going straight through it
The pain, so cruel, is coming to a theater near you.

30. The Sorrow of June

I am sorry…
  For the disappointment I have displayed,
I draw nothing more than a cloud,
Hovered in the center without warning,
  I feel that my life is scorn,
    With disappointment
      And regret,

Forget about me,
  I am still the man you see,
  Just now in your dreams,
An ugly face of misery that deems
Nothing but sorrow and displacement in my plight
Fear not,
  For I have nothing left to fight,
    And I am ready to die…

Don't ask why
  It was simply my time
  Even if I might inflict the pain,
All I can say, is I am sorry,
  For being insane
  There is no one to blame
    Just the rain of tears,
My only fear,
  Left to you,
Kind of blue,

I feel that my life,
Was simply,
      Due…

Time,
   The enemy of my pain
   The girl that never came
The window that held one pane…

Enclosed to the world,
Imprisoned to the joy,
   I wish I was more,
   I wish I could adore,
      One million,
But like a chameleon,
   I am disguised,
      To no one's surprise,
If you ever looked into my eyes,
   You would see the deep sadness of me,
   And know that I could hide no longer
   The day drew longer, and longer,
      And night,
   Sang a sad song,
      Where I belong,

Without a coat, in the storm
   Without peace, in a war
      Without a feast, to form

A shadow at night
This is the time
    I make it right!

Tonight,
    I will kill, all that is a burden
    To ones whom I love,
    I will pull the curtain,
        And close the show
            All I know
                Is that the pain will never go…

Away!
No matter how I pray!
Or what I say!
This sorrow will only stay!

I am sorry,
    For the love,
        I could never convey.

31. The Death of a Wiseman

"Salvation is the key," the wise man says with stone
"Wisdom is the fee," the wise man says all alone
"Believe in your dreams," the wise man says with atonement
"Deny your reason," the wise man says with a lone breath

The wise man see's, but doesn't have sight
The wise man believes, in the birth of the afterlife
The wise man hints, of the risks we all take
The wise man knows, it is your heart you must break

"Listen to me, my son," he states, moving closer to console
"You must know when to leave," he states closer to anole
"And you must know," he pauses, taking a deep breath,
"When to stay," he closes his eyes,
      Whispering his last breath.

32. Burning the Past

Still, waiting to puncture my veins
An injection of pure evil
My dreams fail to the cracks of indecision for which I knew
Or my eyes rest outside my window,
    Dreaming of ocean water blue,

    Daydreaming of the hole, filling white clouds
Hearing the songs, of the robins spring
I never wanted to be a needle
The silence is deafening, you bring

Days pass after another,
She is just a picture on my wall
Reminding me of when I was in love
This picture, my mind can only recall.

33. My Angel of Love

It is warmth that you will never lose
Carrying a smell once receptive that you never forget
Will I see her tonight?
A mystery of her unpredictable life, I ponder
Closing my eyes, angelic sight belongs to her…

    My angel of love,
        Dear angel of mine,
Won't you come to me, and begin our life.

34. From Kansas

She was born, on the first of January
As an angel entered this world
Born was a diamond
And a new state bird

The holiday she flew, to a new direction
For what is behind that smile, came her creation

Waltzing into my life, crossing the English Channel
From the Port of Dover, the observation deck is where I stood
Off flew my hat, as the cold wind blew
A Yankee with pride, if only I could
Not going to lose my loyalty, my hat stopped at a pair of heels
Beige, my eyes slowly gendered above
And it was the first time in my life
That I knew the definition of love

Green eyes, with a smile to hand back my cap
A simple glance turned into a stare that warmed my soul
She stayed next to me, forever inside
Like a diamond in the sky, or a last taxi ride

My lily, a Kansas daisy I pluck for you
Let us walk around Paris, in this moment of time
This is the story,
    Of the day she was mine!

35. *Quandary of Love*

Close to the roots for which my blood runs
Down the river, I float down with my eyes closed
To the banks of heaven, I slowly drift
Until I find no closure, this life I choose

My life comes at a long tide
For which the river cannot reach
I float down the stream for miles
With each mile, I cannot fall asleep

A dream and a destiny for which I am
The place and time, for what I have become
This river runs deep; my heart is cold and numb

Without a soul, my heart is black as night
Does she think about me, or am I lost
Constructed a relationship, deep in my mind
The love of my life, at what cost

7 years ago, she could have been mine
I ride down this river alone, with regret
7 years, close to my destiny and dream
I close my eyes to only regret.

36. The Wind

The wayward direction of the aimless psyche
Disillusioned by the automatic and relentless society
Of the pain for which directions traveled are bestowed
It was the start of a fire, which only the wind knows

Only the wind...
Only the wind can grasp the departure of days and night
The sun and the moon come and go without a fight
You lose sight, on the endless wonderment of the conflicted
We pass with the wind, and it comes unpredicted

It was the wind...
We fought for the ability to spark a fire
A place and a time, where nature calls to the loathing

> *Wind, it slowly begins blowing.*

37. Duality

If you only knew, the truth of my life
You'd understand the depths of romance I fall
Then imagine, you would drink with me at the bar
Ignore my pleads most withdrawal

As just another man and not a man of extreme desire
Wishing they would simply look into my eyes, and know the truth
Yet I hide from her warranted expression of distaste
Walking away, I watch her grow distant to my color blue

Tears never falling, leaving my eyes heavy, and unburdened with life...
Sedation is my only reservation whenever I think about the night
What could have been, or simply what never happened
I will let you guess, while I laugh heartedly inside,

To all those, with my name in their mouth,
Keep it the same, and won't ever doubt,
The ignorance of bliss,
Uninformed intuition, I blow you a kiss

If only you knew...
That I laugh outside,
When the depths of my pain,
Leaves me to die.

38. Whispers of the Sea

I leave the comforts of my own town
The place I live in through time confound
Deep in the ocean, your boat sails in the direction of the wind
To another island, I begin to travel the seas within

Supplies stored, my destination mapped, compass was set,
With waves that pour, the rain drops down my neck
Only time left, to songs of the water, boat I sail south,
Live your charter, rum and red stripe down my mouth

A son of a son of a sailor, out on the sea for adventure
Buffet told me to claim truth in your ventures
Through trains, planes, automobiles – the sea tells no lies
Leaving the comforts of life to find morality undefined

In touch with Mother Nature, and father sky's test
Spotting the white sand beaches, soft grains until reaching rocks quest
My feet adore, in the ruins of socks
Where I greeted a Native of land clocked

"How long did you listen to the waves," he asked
I told him, "Long enough to know why I am here,"
"Welcome to paradise," I was told,
A place in my mind I never will grow old.

39. Tired of the Streetlight

Walking down the road of life
With sunglasses on, during the night
With a path empty to travel
Tired of the streetlight

Tired of being concerned for what I cannot control
Tired of anxiety and suicidal thoughts
Tired of everyone doubting me
Tired of all the battles I fought

I walk down the road of life
Sunglasses on, during the night
With a path empty from uncertainty
Tired of the streetlight

Tired of being stabbed in the back
Tired of being so alone
Walking an empty path
Searching for a golden stone

While I walk down the road of life
Sunglasses to shade, the moon at night
A path filled with desperate expressions
I ignore the streetlight
That I always fight
The difference between wrong and right.

40. The Great American Love Song

It was truly destiny, and truly fate
For you to come into my life, with so much at stake
When you can't tell the difference between real and fake
Blowing out the birthday candles on my cake

Changing by the calendar of time
This year, I wish to find
A passionate lover, I was slowly dying
Alone and crying,

From the one that got away
Thinking for what I could say
In my bed of wonderment is where I lay
Letting the rain turn the mud into clay

This is the great American love song
Praying for a love that is gone
Infinite and true to where I belonged
In a love song, I question...

Will I find my fate?
Will my dreams come true?
I already know,
I'm in love with you.

41. The Manifestation of Time and Love

Look at the image of Shiva and Goddess
Living in a cave of light
Shut your eyes
Imagine them
Shining, alive, glorified
Manifested

How beautiful
The depths of tenderness
Wisdom spoken beyond all dictation
That sensual experience
Spiritual fusion and atonement
Manifested

Eternity
In love with time
Joined in marriage
United with one
Nirvana, Samsura
The manifestation of time and love

42. Direction is born

The cult followed the Sheppard,
The Sheppard followed the sheep
The sheep chase the dream,
That would never let him sleep

God damn those sheep, why won't they leave!
Maybe the Sheppard, really couldn't see
As the cult kept on marching, onward to oblivion
The path was not clear, let us follow the sun.

43. The Storyteller

The falling clouds come tumbling down,
Collapsing is your soul, silence told the sound,
Be alone, not lonely, are both sides of the coin
As the falling clouds come tumbling down,

Heads or tails, the equality inside of a contradiction,
The falling clouds, a simple search for benediction,
All alone, inside a crowded room, silence will pretend,
Telling the falling sky, for the story to begin…

44. Pick Up The Phone

I was gazing out of the window, of the St James Hotel
Picking up the phone, there is no one there
So alone, surrounded by a crowd of people to the door
I can't get past, left love once and now sore

Looking off the edge off the cliff, nearly dead from pity and despair
So cold and alone, love left a trail of crumbs to compare
When your heart fell, leaving my stomach to knots and stone
I kept leaving love; to ring again and again, hang up the phone

There is no one there, knocking on a door of uncertainty,
It opens to the past, love will come, my princess to be
Personally with subversively acting, nothing at all
It was left to gravity, when the last domino falls

So I gazed out the window, so cold and so alone,
Searching for someone to love me, but they never picked up the phone.

45. Flight around the Sun

Oh, what web we all weave, I can remember age seventeen
A circle of excess, along with all the lustful pleasures you dream
For when only you arrive, in that next in age
Another flight around the sun, or a story in a page

The circumference we roll, I recommend the age twenty one
Living for the moment, all the possibility I've done
Yet when you arrive, to that next day
Another flight around the sun, maybe you'll learn someday

About the indigestion, beginning at the age of twenty five
You look tepid at the bar, just another night
And when you arrive, to that next sight
Just a flight around the sun, without winking an eye

Finally reached, the age of twenty seven
Looking back, you laugh, knowing you'd rolled eleven
In the circle you spun, to be at this page
One flight around the sun, it seemed so strange,
  But I wouldn't trade my life, for even one page.

46. A Vacation of Wine

From the city of Bordeaux, was the red French taste of wine?
In Germany we climb, the grapes of Riesling from off the vine
Growing in the city of Chianti, Italy is a place I wish to explore
A nice pinot noir, Sonoma County from which I adore

The palate of ecstasy, in the mind of a vintner
You must forgive my taste; it's the sweetest wine I remember

Roses, growing from the soil, in a South African field
Of going to Australia, to experience the city of Shiraz concealed
Pinot Gringo grows like chardonnay, an American state of California wine
A 2009 Argentinean wine you purchase, to simply see what you'll find

My palate of bliss, amongst my mind is a French vintner
I regret none of my taste, for the sweetest wine to remember
All I can do is dream of the grape vines,
Amongst the season of December…

47. Winter Song

The winter air howls through the crack in my basement window
Screaming with the intent of a bitterly frozen storm,
With the wind swirling the snow into a tornado
I stay below, as I shiver, dreaming of warmth

It was the first snow of the season
And I cried with the winds of destiny
Tears falling down into the pit of my stomach
I cannot treasure that which I cannot see

These howls continue, with more vigor and fright
A numbing cold sunrise, awakening to the weeping souls
Lost in the middle, not passing up to heaven

For my death is coming with the winter breeze
Chilling and dark, like the blackness before the dawn
Devoid of any righteousness or credence
I listen to the cold souls singing this song.

48. Treasure Chest

I have built a treasure chest, locked away,
Swallowing the only key to open the door
You must pass through to get past this plight
And look beyond, not look before

Is it trinkets of gold, silver or cash?
Or could it be a box of old pictures
Maybe all my lost love letters,
It might become the lost scriptures

Of the holy testament of God
He speaks through these words of despair
Without a face, nor name, he becomes present
As he rocks in the oldest of rocking chairs

Swaying back and forth, I swallowed the only key
Only the man that lives in the clouds
Will know what the treasures are
When this sonnet is unlocked and found.

49. Survive

Starring at the dark spaces, deep within the closet
The countless reaction, of the tick of the clock
Tick-tock, I stare, deep with tranquility
sooner or later, I lost the truth of ability

Apathy was in the heart, with the mind of liberty
Deep within your heart, I find nothing but tranquility
Fighting within, you can look away, the shadow
You cannot remember, stepping on the ladder

Climbing a hill, I lift the trance of a daze
And fall backwards, with my arms ablaze
The truth of ability, is that it takes time
With your life frail, you must first survive

50. Memory of her Scent

I love the smell of your hair, letting me know spring is here
And the flowers begin to bloom, textured leaves of fur
Let us open the window, shut off the thermostat, let God exhale
Nature of the sun, the stars and the moon,
To dwell in heaven...

I close my eyes, and her scent lingers on,
    It's been five years...
        Five years...

That was the last time I saw her face, her smile, her eyes,
Green, to see for the first time, as Blind Man Davis
It is a picture that fire cannot burn,
Nor will scissors cut,
For it stays,
    The lingering love...

Oh, how I miss her scent...

It's finally gone,
I wish it would return; dejected, there is solace in her picture,
A dream I often had,
A dream that was once true,
A dream of paradise on earth,
The dream was you...

Emotions, as I miss the pain
I cannot remove her aroma, opening the window in December,
Without her, I cannot part
    Yet, her scent is not willing to leave my heart.

51. The First Snow

As my hair grows longer, it is the beginning of the first snow of the year
You see no clouds, only flakes of ice dropping from the sky to appear
Seeing the difference only takes a device with what memories feared
Believing within us simply breaks the ice of the first snow drop as a tear

52. On the Farm

The history of rhythm starts with the lyrical verse,
Finding an inner-connection among the epidemic curse
Found with even a pale gesture
Music was created, along an empty pasture

53. Café' Stevens

Inside the Café' Stevens, in Amsterdam
Sipping a cup of coffee, tranquil, I am
Lost inside a mind of contradictory
Finding solace, in every smile I see

Inside the Café' Stevens, in Amsterdam
Bob Dylan plays on the juke box, sinking in the sand
I'm lying along the beach, with a Heineken
Was this a revolution, I started to begin

Inside the Café' Stevens, in Amsterdam
A poet without a muse, learning cultural stands
Lost inside a mind, that is sinking into sand
Finding solace, she held my hand

54. Gray Sky Turned Blue

The Café' Poco Loco, seemed innocent
From first glance, I inhaled the jasmine scent
So I entered with a grin, drinking a cup of brew
Things were pretty lovely; the gray skies seemed blue

I finally crossed the pond, a rainy day in Holland
So I entered the Café' Poco Loco, a drink to swallow
The longer I stayed, the more I knew
Those things were pretty lovely; the grey skies seemed blue

So many questions I must answer with conviction
Maybe the Café' Poco Loco, will bring me benediction
Yearning to find that which I define as true
All I know, is that today, the grey skies turned blue

55. City of Red

My memory clouds my judgment, it's allowed
The depths of the city, a lustful crowd
Temptations got a hold, not letting go
I transcend into a place that nobody knows

A cloudy day, mixed with a rainy street
Walking down Zeeduk, I follow my feet
Temptations grasp is constricting, not letting go
Mapping out a trace, learning the word no

Lost in grey skies, deep with the clouds
Wandering a sinful path, it's allowed
Temptation is pushing me to the edge
In the heart of the city of red

56. My November Rain

Back at Pacific Beach, onto a November rain
Today I turned another age, something else to blame
Than the time apart, I find a way
Let upon, the morning dew each day

Back at the water, watching the weather fall
I see that this age, will never learn at all
Runners end up walking, left astray
I find a way, to be the morning dew each day

Touching the sand, water through my toes
Today I turned an age, only two of us know
All the time apart, I always find a way
To walk through the cold November rain

57. 29 Years, 29 Ways

In the ten o'clock hour, sitting amongst the rest of the beach dwellers
On my 29th birthday, the clock turns, as I sit fortunate to tell ya
The morning ticks, like a ripple, once a wave from the pacific
Growing to ponder at the Green Tea Leaf, for a cappuccino they deliver

Gazing along the boardwalk, one surfs or blades
For ocean water never touched, my feet fell astray
California love, with a poet's heart
While I watch the waves, that always start

Will I wake, from this immaculate dream?
Or stay lost, amongst the Green Tea Leaf
Once a year, I am, for this to begin
But I must start, only where I know, at the end

58. Real or Fake

Roses emerge, are they real or are they fake
Letting out a sigh, with not another mistake
I gave up years ago, while ears still wet
Only this day comes to not regret

The seagulls that swoop, downward and in
In their behalf, they are clueless to their end
Like me, I find, another tale told
Free and alive, on a pathless road

Tranquility comes, in the depths of insanity
Free-will is a belief, I am yet to see
Or understand, whether real or fake
All I know, is that beauty is never a mistake

59. No Country

I am a man with no country
I am a man with no home
I am a man with no placement
I am a man left to roam

The lands of the earth, beauty of the sky
Laying brick after brick, creation I intend
To live life as a man with no country, no home
Just a man, that God left to roam

Find solace in the daily pleasures, the ticks from the clock
Life is an untraveled road, lessons we believe in
I am a man with no country, a man left to roam
Just a man laying bricks that will all turn to stone?

A man with no county
A man with no home
Will I find placement?
Only God knows

60. Penny in the Well

I fell in love with a girl, her name was Audrea
She was from Sweden, walked into my life today
Native tongue that drew me near; yet, I fell
Making love in my mind, just another penny in the well

61. The Frost

A morning walks through the snow
How the cold wind blows,
    In this town, I find lost
    Searching to begin
    I feel December,
        Through the frost

62. And Tonight's Special is…

I come from far and away
The 2 o'clock hour, has led me to stray
For in she walks, and here I wait
To make my move, I see my prey

I will slowly walk, when out she leaves
A boxing match, I bob as she weaves
But I don't follow her, I sit and I wait
For she smelled my scent, and she is the bait

Walking outside, to smoke and see
God damn almighty, the possibility
She follows the worm, the bite is near
All it takes is a word, a mouth not to fear

And out it comes, what a glorious sport
What is your name, to which I retort?
Next a laugh, then a backhanded compliment
It isn't long, for her clothes I will strip

Up to my room, my meal has arrived
First a kiss with a touch, no longer to survive
Smooth as silk, my mouth starts to salivate
As this fine female, on tonight's dinner plate

63. She Loves Me

Words spoken without a sound
Untold conversations all between
Finding fortune and satisfaction
I have all that is needed

64. Onto a New

Looking for an ocean view
Learning twice, through and through
If the time told, you would only knew
That this too will pass, and onto a new

65. Waiting for the Tide

A pocketful of sand, asleep at the beach
Closer to the sun, in a paradise I reach
Waiting for the tide, to touch my toes,
With the rising sun below my nose

Central to the moon, I write a letter
Living in the sub-conscious, beyond matter
Now, a pocketful of grass, I lay in the field
Closer to the stars, how their distance won't yield

Waiting for the tide, to reach my toes
Among the sun, rising beneath my nose
A pocket full of rocks, alone in a ditch,
In the sublime of eternal bliss

As I wait for the tide, to reach my toes,
When will it come?
    Only God knows.

66. The Immigrant

The bar begins to crowd, a variety of flavors to choose
Brown hair, blue eyes, tall or short, BB playing the blues
Singing in the background, nothing less than brilliant
A place filled with royalty, I was just an immigrant

67. Only the Thief

Take my body, for my spirit will live
Learn to forgive, the melancholy rhythm of life
Without insanity, learning the humanity,
    Of man, selfish with pity,
Only the thief understands…
    A life without dignity

68. To Hear Her Footsteps

Her footsteps were no more, I adore
Such a sentimental mood, you held me consumed
In the gluttony of lust, it was her I trust
Falling into her arm,
    Is sure to be my doom…
        So I loom…

In remembrance, my memorial
No longer green or red, without pain
I take a deep breath, until there is nothing left
If I am lucky,
    I will hear her footstep

69. Find Comfort

One more cup of coffee for the road
Black, with one ice cube
I sip in the dark of night
Blind to a care in sight

Can I have a smoke before you go?
Highway 35 west, I must know
To the deserts and seas I roam
Not a care in the world
      To cross my soul

Take one shot
Don't let the road pass you by
Live your life with honor
Never a question why

Drink to honesty
For it is all true
One more cup of coffee for the road
And let god bless you

70. Mysterious Nights

Whatever comes when darkness falls?
Happily ever after
Or nothing at all
The sun will rise
Left only to fall
The mystery of the night
To the heavens we saw

71. Shooting Star

Oh, shooting star, shooting star
You seem so far, where ever you are going
Please grant my wish
    Where ever you are...

Oh, shooting star, shooting star
Why are you so far, don't leave me
At least grant me my wish
    Where ever you are...

Oh, shooting star, shooting star
From above so far, where ever you fall
Please grant my wish,
Love, whenever she calls

72. Winter Wind

7 A.M.
Waking to the wind
Blowing through my open hotel window
The coldest air I would befriend

73. Create the Day

Breakfast
Bread caked with sugar
Powdered I believe
The most important meal of the day
In me was conceived

74. Boy from Kansas

A boy from Kansas, such starry night
The love affair with beauty, can be such a cold delight
Walking amongst the streets, that have no names
Just take one look, each one feels the same

So he boarded a jet, to Europe to find
Somehow, somewhere, a pure piece of mind
Maybe a love, he can call his own
To take her back, to his Kansas home

Prague was where he landed, and anonymous he was
These beautiful ladies that roam, just because
It was his love affair with beauty, such a cold fright
This boy from Kansas, may he find it tonight

75. You

I must confess, I am in love with you!
Hair golden blonde, and eyes so blue
Falling for no other, and this is true
My heart belongs to only one,
    And that is you

76. Chasing a Shadow

Our destination may be far apart
But my indifference will never start
Won't you hold my heart?
    Not letting it fall apart

Can you not see?
    We were meant to be
At last
I caught up to my past

Chasing this shadow
Surviving the battle
For she will never be caught
    So here I run,
        Chasing what cannot be caught

77. Dawn

What is there to say, upon a wintery day?
Clouds so grey,
    It makes you wonder…
        What is dawn to a day?

78. The Scent that Lingers

It has been over 2 years, since I have seen her face
Yet I can still smell her skin, on my tongue I taste
The whispery pines blow, and with it the shivers of the wind
Yet I can still feel the warmth
    Of her angelic skin

79. Recipe for Love

A dash of glowing shadows
A taste of seasoned strawberries
Washed down by the champagne of freedom
A Sunday morning, looking outward past 10,000 acres
Wheat that harvest this morning, waiting breakfast
The tongue tells the moments that cannot break us

80. Knowing Where to End

Johnny Walker, red label, or at least I thought it was,

After this night, blended scotch, would hold no more, and I am lost, on six, par 3, can you see, 145 yards; should of used an 8 iron, my lye is rough, and through all this, I see the hole is not so near!

Shot after shot, I skip the green, let the club do the work, finally reaching the end, as I approach the hole, to fall into your reason for existence, the natural effect of this cause comes to a conclusion, without solution…

Towards this red label, or at least I thought it was; yet after this life, I only fall, would hold no more, on the number six, and fragility of my shot, must be blended scotch…

Knowing where to end,
Or so I thought

81. Everything

The tinted shade fluttered through the venetian blinds, and I thought of you...

A long enduring memory, I could see your smile across the sunset over a Wheatfield in the town of Americus, I thought of the only blunders I felt fumbling arraignment I have with this world...

Such a sorrow felt regret, our time was pleasant, but I must confess: this is what must stay, a long enduring memory of you...
My love....
My joy...
My sorrow...
My pain...
My sun...
My moon...

You are everything that is good in my life!

82. I Live in Casablanca

Casablanca, it fell to escape
But the trap of love left a heart to break
The 3rd Reich came, and the 3rd Reich captured
Escaping from France, the ominous rapture

Danger, no politics allowed
Opinions of love, a simple cloud
A dream, a kiss is just a kiss
I am in-between,
    That trust
        I yearn to kiss

83. If I could Have you

I stare deep into a crowded room
But there is only one soul I see
The beauty glowing a spectrum
My soul is closer,
        Can it be?

For the plight of your future
Wedding bells ring
To fall into your arms
Is our destiny

Slowly, with a kiss
Time is eternal
With you, there is no death
Only a commercial

If I could have you
Slowly, in your arms
I would love those drums
If I could have you
Slowly with temperance

84. My First Line to You

My knees have fallen
In the ground, the endless ground
Our time apart
Is a never ending sound

85. The Morning Fire

Put a candle in the wind
    I am bound to drift awhile,
Let me float up in the clouds
One by one, step by step
    You take me beyond the sky
Think of me, when the sun also rises
I hide my comfort in a shell hardened by a society,
    Jealous and envious…

Still, the hummingbird sings
    A song of content
    A song of plight
    A song of rebirth
That ends,
    Blowing out the lights

86. Will and Self

The values we hold on the common household
Separation of the will from the self, a deadly poison
Swallowed by those who hold inhumane principles
That of which they live, and sin without regard
A continuation of the upcoming Armageddon
Man has manifested through his own ego
Psych, unknown, yet fearful to the simplicity
Remembering that Satan comes with a smile
And the biggest trick he ever staged,
> Was to convince the world he never existed…

We should never turn away from the basic human right,
That comes from the will, and for which our self tells at night

87. Dressed In Mud

Results are always perfect
Please, try again
Test squandering a temptation
Learning how to sin

Waking up without a god
Waking up without a prayer
Alone, with a sickening grin
Dressed in shame I bare

The humble hearted boy
In a grief stricken world
A night without loyalty
As the sun became a blur

To never hold guilt
Deep inside a conscience mind
Without a conscious soul
To leaving it all behind

A way to sin
And a way to laugh
With a body full of water
Cleansing my heart with a bath

That takes away the pain
Of being young and dumb
Saying what I don't mean
Or what I have become

When this new day comes
Results are perfect to dream
If I could only feed off the pen
My life would be utopic to me

Impeccable, without a stain
I wash away the blood
Starring down the drain
Moment's I dressed in mud

88. A Red Heaven

I love the high you give me
When you are lying next to me in bed
Your soul touching mine
Floating in a heaven that's red

I would give my life
Just so you could have one more day
I would sacrifice my expression
Just to taste your lips today

With nothing but time to ignore
By my side through every mistake
All I own is love
Every time my dreams would create

You stood by my side
Through thick and thin
You were more than a lover
You are my greatest friend

I trusted you with certainty
Never doubting the warmth you read
You are my shadow on the wall
We live in a heaven that is red

89. Sea of Blue

In the sea of blue, 8th inning,
*   Royals 6, Athletics 7,*
*   29 years, without a crown they lived*
Sitting with annex of a fan never knowing
Having the temperance of fate,
*   We all live… they just fight…*
So here come the Royals,
*   And you cannot stop them on this night*

90. At Night

I see in her eyes, a smile I haven't seen
Knowing you are in love, is living in the dream
Her eyes
Her lips
    I miss her ways
Why can't I just
Turn the page

What I see in her eyes, a smile of joy and ecstasy
I know I am in love, is learning to believe
In her heart
Her soul
    I miss the way
She finds my holes
Deep within my soul

What I hold in her eyes, with a face of warmth and clarity
So in love with you, I can hardly believe
I found you
My love
    I miss each passing second
You are gone from my sight

Deep in my soul, I turn the page, to the still of the night

91. November Rain

Back at Pacific Beach, onto a November rain
Today I turned another age, something else to blame
The time apart, I find my way
Let up on this morning dew of a new day

Back at the water, watching the weather fall
I see that this age, will never learn at all
Runners ending up walking left astray
Finding a way, to be the morning dew each day

Touching in sand, water in between my toes
Today I turned another age, only 2 of us know
All the time apart, I always find a way
To walk through, the cold dew of an April day

92. Vernal Equinox

In a winter weather advisory
It has not snowed all year
On the first day of spring
I feel as if I no longer belong in this place
The sun begins to fall
    As the night comes with a chill
The cold air whistling through my front door singing a lonely song
Depressive to the day the seed began to grow
Frozen in the ground
    With 7 inches of snow

93. The End is Close

These days that I live with doubt
These days, I live without…

Such a fallacy that poetics played
All the jeans I wear are frayed
Wishing that you could have stayed
Instead, I prayed

For you, my lord; in a time of uncertainty
When a man can destroy the world; with the push of a button…we
Bask in the rays of the sun to live so free
To write about the days, expression came to me

From strength and determination, I always find
When I fear that time is passing me by
The end is near, for the lord I cry
That my body will perish, but my soul will never die

In these days after this poem I bleed
These days, in our time of need
In these days, I predicted and said
My days, that I spent dreaming of the color red
    Instead
        Of grey

On these days,
    These days I pray

94. Consideration

Always tell the truth
Don't eat the last appetizer before offering it
Tell your destination
Be punctual, be respectful of even those opinions that you disagree with
Put yourself last in line to receive
Clean what you dirty
Fix what you break
Admit your weaknesses, and when you are wrong
Honesty is the key
Charitable contributions to those whom are in need
That opens the door to "Gods" truths…

Humans are animals,
    And,
        Don't gamble your life away

(Taught by my mother)

95. The Four Women

Chelsea, oh my dear, Chelsea
With your hair flying in the wind
Blonde and beautiful, is the sight of my endeavor
Locking at your bliss, defines that you are forever
In my mind, in my eyes, and in my dreams
You are,
    Tonight,

Ardis, oh my dear, Ardis
Your body moves with grace
I look deep within your blue eyes
Seeing way beyond your face
Watching your soul, spin like a star
Ardis, my dear
    Wherever you are

Alice, oh my dear, Alice
With your fingers licking the bowl
You bake a cake each night, just to see me full
Frosting on your face, I lick it off your hand, bit by bit
Alice, my dear
    You are hard to forget

Katie, oh my dear, Katie
You beauty is so clear, your body so warm
You leave me without fear
That white dress, I cannot ignore

Firmly but gently holding your body against me
Katie, my dear
      How I adore

These are,
Four women of my life
Four women of my time
Four women I will never know
The four women I will never find

96. Season of fall

The lightning piercing the sky
Leaving me without the comfort of electricity
I light 8 candles, o enter a glow at sight
With this storm at six in the morning
The sun awaits the night

I ponder at the rain, falling hard to the ground
The rumbling sky, I felt awkward
To the collision, to the ground
You find a flight in the terrain
Tomorrow will never be found

Whilst, the green is slowly turning to brown
With patterns of the drains trickling down

The season has passed, and a new arrives
With a path of contemptuous song
The thunder rolling, this fall

97. The Circle of Life

Rain remains on the branch of the trees
That someday will fall
It clings to the bark,
    With the grasp of God,
Knowing that eventually,
    It will eventually drop

And sink into the soil for a new beginning
A rebirth
Blades of green grass

Or maybe a hayfield,
So content with its pastures,
Becoming unbridled life

98. Temptation

Harmony squanders herself short of my door,
I walk my hallway, and all but ignore
Passing by, my every glance of love and lust
I'd carefully drive, but to walk, I must learn to trust

My footsteps make a heavy echo
With each pressing of my heel
I could not catch my breath
So desperate to feel

I must,
Follow the treasures of a bountiful journey
I kiss the wife and kids goodbye
For they know that I will be true
In the time, our heart decides
To be colored,
      Black and blue

99. Feathers

Get busy living, or get busy dying?

This birds land is near with fright
Colors of an array sparkle upon us brought about safety
      Amongst the birds flight

He lands, unblemished, and I swear I saw a smile
He looks up to the Gods for whom he obliges
The Lord saw his bright feathers
And saved this birds life,
    From this March weather

100. Blue Eyes

Those blue eyes, I swim so deep, like the ocean off the Bahamas
The window into her soul, they tell me her heart pleads
To feel true love, and shared amongst all
Her presence brings me weak in the knees, to slowly fall

In love with the conception of her life, and my expectations that lie
She is the one, who understands my need to fly
As an artist, her old soul, has lived a life of virginity in love
Purity with each glance, a smile from her must come from above

I love, the way she looks, turning heads
My bed and look ahead, to her
And our plight, man and wife, known tonight
The day we met, I will never forget, out poured the sweat
I slowly checked
If my heart, stayed apart, or it released
From her spark
Glory, glory, beauty and joy, I love her smile
I say a joke, or play a toy, just to enjoy
Her smile, her smile
      Let me embrace it…
           For a little while

101. Beyond Time

A conscious filled with unrelenting dispassion
The distance we stand in order to simply relax
To learn our comfortable acuity in life
Is to know our true ability beyond the night

To be beyond the wind, is to be one with love
living beyond the breeze, we can feel the heaven above
Go ahead, beyond the wind, my soul will burn a fire
I am beyond the wind, left full of desire

It was a conscious you filled with merciless shame
That took you beyond and killed this blissful vein
Triumph to collapse, I find the distance we stand for relaxation
Taking a bath, in the indecision I pretending conservation

Is acuity ever comfortable in life?
With the wind blowing at night
Faced with the contradictions of true love and destiny
Relapse this intuition that trust is a lack of envy

I am beyond the wind, left full with desire
Protection and warmth, I lit the first fire

102. Timeless Age

The November climate brings a bitter cold
Wind blowing off the frozen glass
Leaves falling in a rock filled yard
A chill utters up my spine
      A change is coming
As the winter enters with an early darkness
Why rhyme, time I spent simply unconscious

The years pass, with seasons telling the story
Sun glaring off the dashboard
Roads turned vigilant and outpour age
The hairs rise on my arms
      A change is coming
As spring comes with uncertainty of the season beyond this
With another season, spent in the subconscious

My hair grows longer, as I dive into the ocean
While clouds filter the sun from loneliness
Sand coming to shore as seashells
The warmth undresses my skin
      A change is coming
As the summer air, dry and dusty I breathe
In skin darker, into a black room I retreat

The colors of autumn in Kansas are beauty
Spectrums of diversity with each passing tree
Knowing death is near, the leaves sing
In the bye and by
    A change is coming
As time,
    Keeps going by

103. Often a Dream

I dream of you often
My dear, you are my only love
I will wait for you forever
And know you will be mine
    One day, when the face comes
In the divine

Our time together is sparse
My dear, you are my only love
I will wait for you forever
Knowing you just don't know love
    But one day, when you look for it
My face will come above

Holding hands, strolling down the shore
My dear, you are my only love
Forever I will wait
Knowing you will come to me
    One day, looking for love
Then you will see

My dream, of us often
My dear, in the depths of my arms
Holding you forever
Knowing I was there for every smile
    One day, when you are faced with love
You and I, will learn to fly

104. Conclusion

When we can lift the band aid of war
Peace and love will soar
Bloodshed that come before
For protection, evermore

A trigger can be pulled by anyone without a soul
So easy to kill, a million bodies to roll
In a grave in the desert, for nobody to know
The injustice of war that no cinema can show

Holding your best friend in your arms, as he takes his last breath
Eyes that stare father than the sun, until there is nothing left
Dying for protection, war is defined to me as death
Immoral, unholy, the nightmare without depth

Waking up with a cold sweat of fear
For this day, the end is here
My conclusion is an eternity left clear
The horrors and sins, far and near

These days, these days
Filled with Gods rays
The swing set I often play
These days...
Just a conclusion,
    For these days,
        These days are precious.

Epilogue

I always wanted to be Humphrey Bogart...an American in Casablanca owning a bar where he sticks his head out for no man.... But only one woman! Seclusion to his past, a mystery to his patrons, knowing your passions fold inside your soul, granting serenity in the love you give to the girl you knew in a past life, all in the remembrance that we will always have Paris. Laying in the Tuileries Jardine below the Eifel Tower, surrounded by a prism of overnight that sparkles of every shade of the leaves that slowly fall of the oaks amongst a Kansas autumn! Dropping to the ground, we lay side by side; staring up at the elephant shape clouds of our destiny, and in it lays a certainty that can only be defined as love.

Oh, how I yearn to know this feeling!

And yet, I dream of the possibilities of the future, and must say goodbye...

We'll always have Paris...

uct-compliance